HOW TO CREATE YOUR ORNAMENTS

It's never been easier to make your own Christmas ornaments. With the dozens of die-cut patterns provided, you'll be able to color, punch out, and assemble a tree's worth of trimmings in no time.

First things first, you'll want to decide what you'll be coloring with. Colored pencils and fine-tip markers will work best for these intricate patterns. If you're going to be using markers, though, it's a good idea to test them on the page outside of the die-cut design. This way you can make sure the ink doesn't bleed through to the other side.

Once you know what you'll be coloring with, it's time to choose the perfect colors for your personalized ornaments. Be sure to select colors that not only complement one another, but also complement the other decorations you have on and around your tree. Pair red and green for a traditional look, or go monochromatic in shades of wintry blue. You can make your designs pop with metallic pens or markers, bringing gold and silver highlights to the ornaments. Or break out the glue stick and glitter once you've finished coloring and make everything sparkle. It's all up to you!

Each ornament consists of two pieces with the same pattern. After you've colored both sides of each piece, it's time for the super-easy assembly. Punch out both pieces of the ornament along the perforated lines. Then line up the slot at the top of Piece B with the slot at the bottom of Piece A and insert Piece B into Piece A.

Thread a short length of string or ribbon through the hole at the top, tie it into a bow, and there you go—your very own homemade Christmas ornament!

A

B

A

B

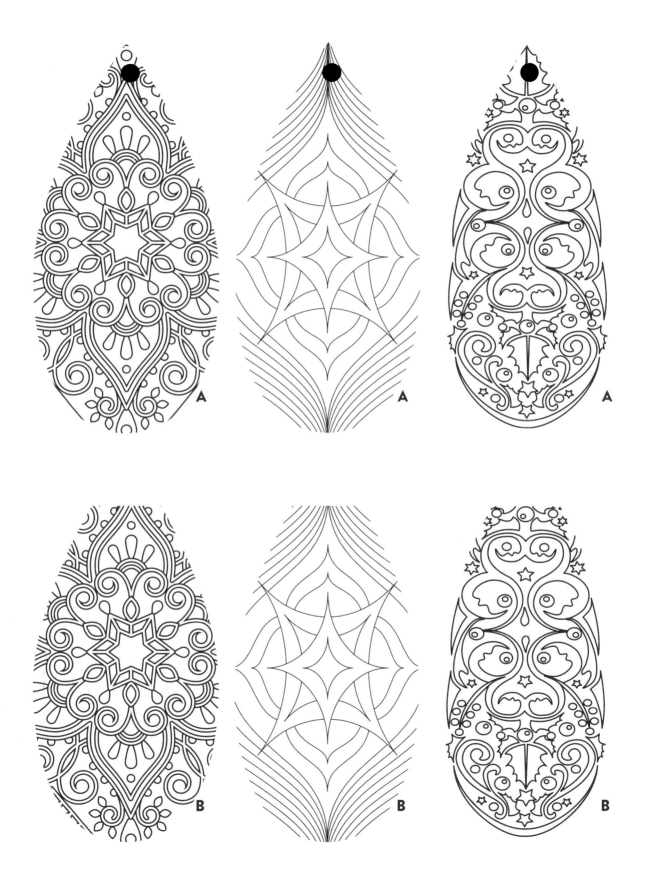

A

A

A

B

B

B

A

B

A

B

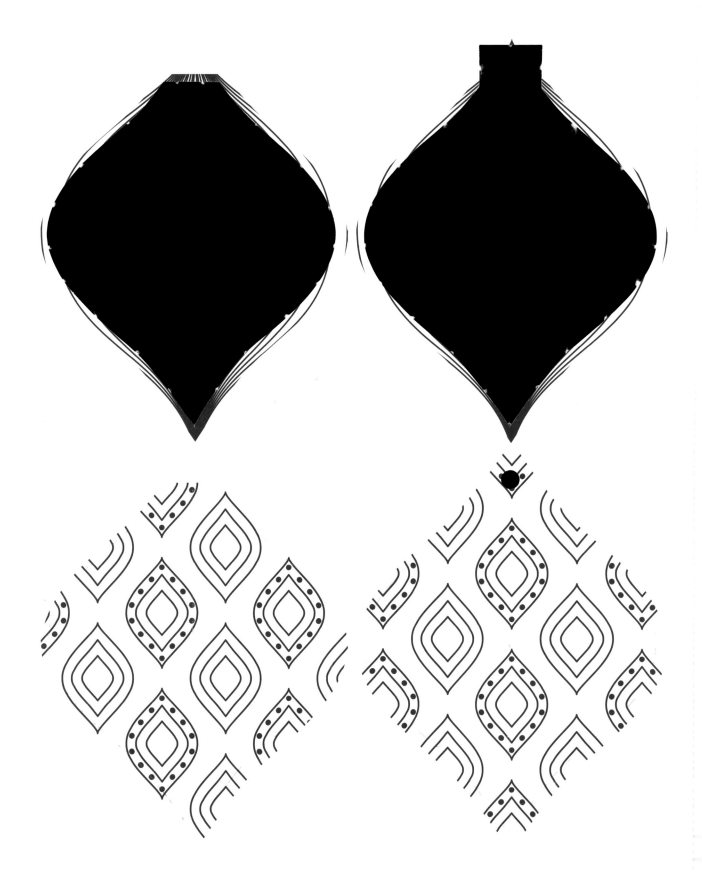

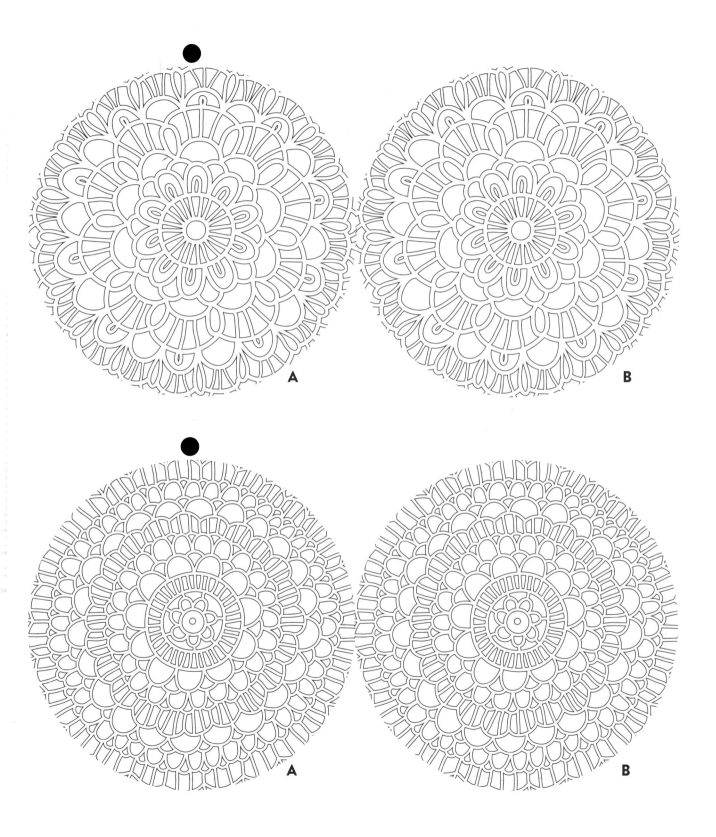

A

B

A

B

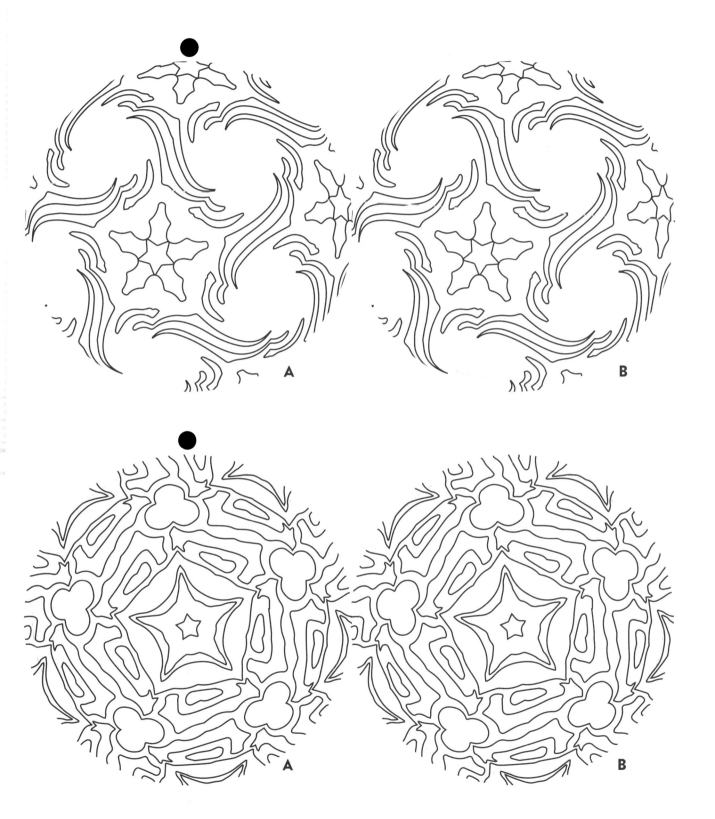

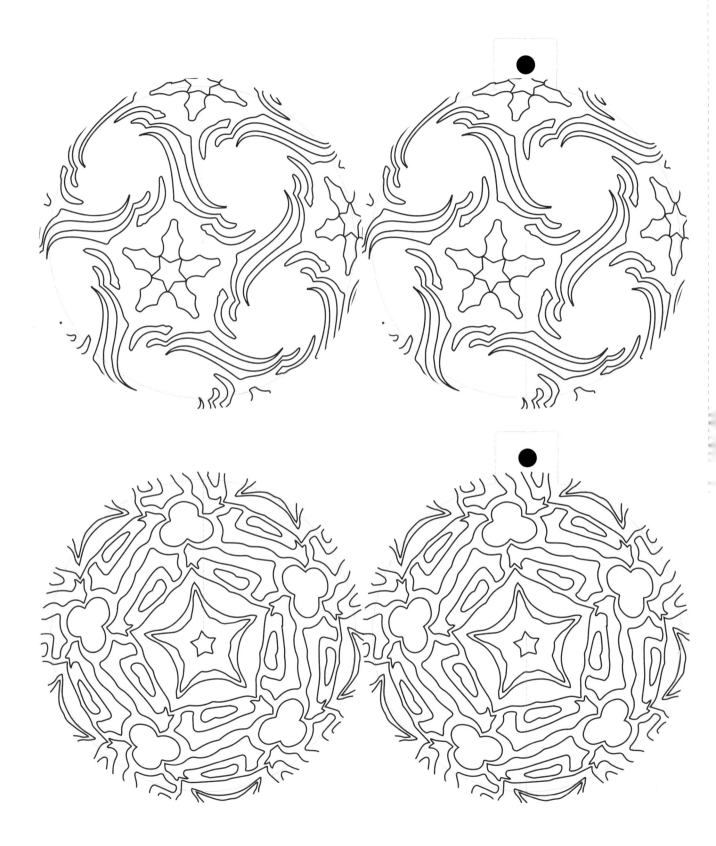

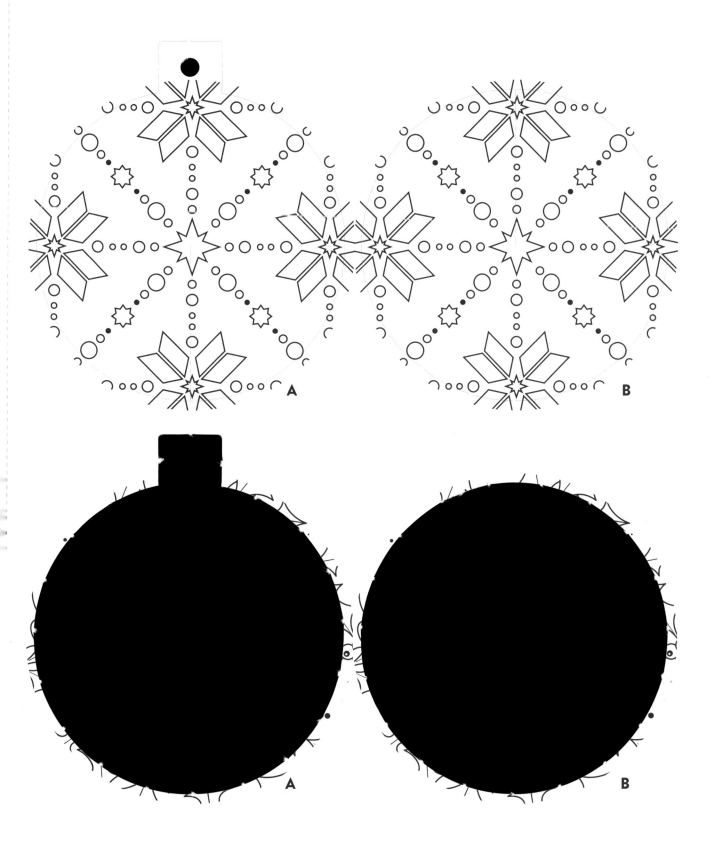

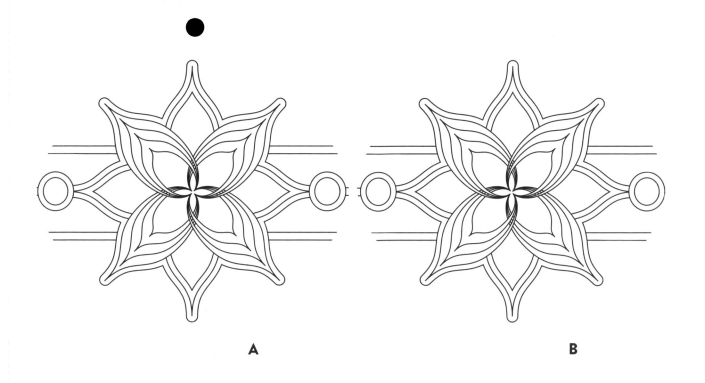

A   B

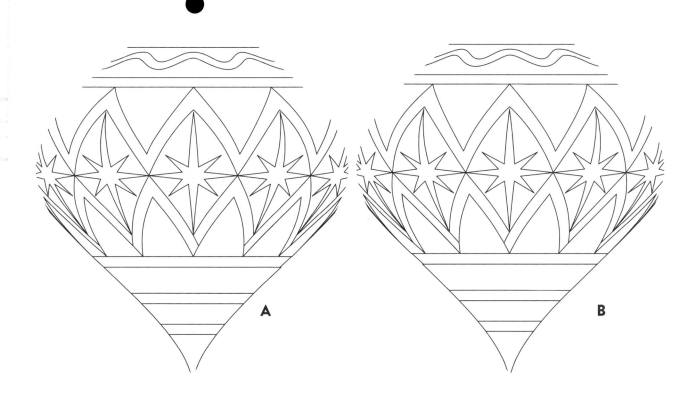

A   B

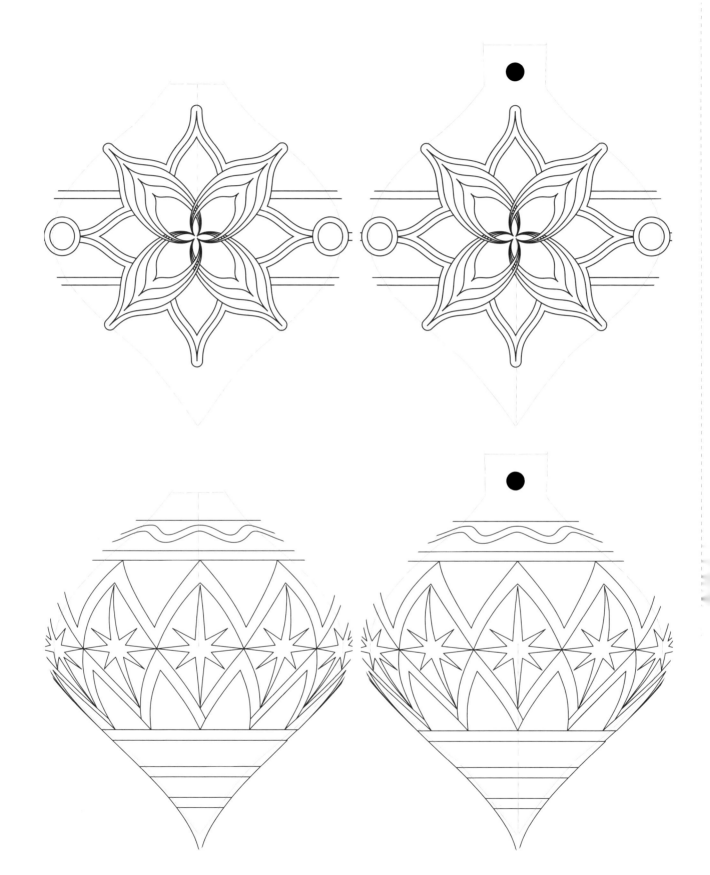

A

B

A

B

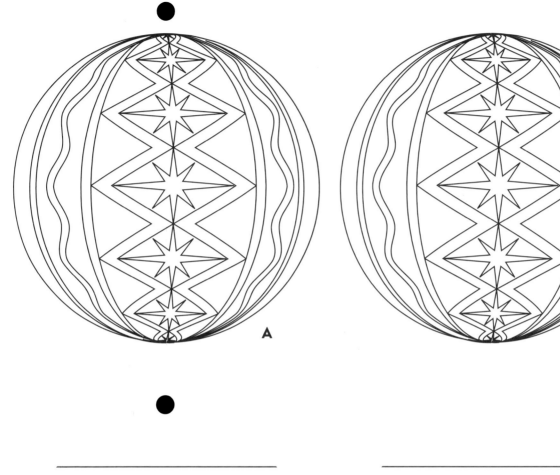

A   B

A   B

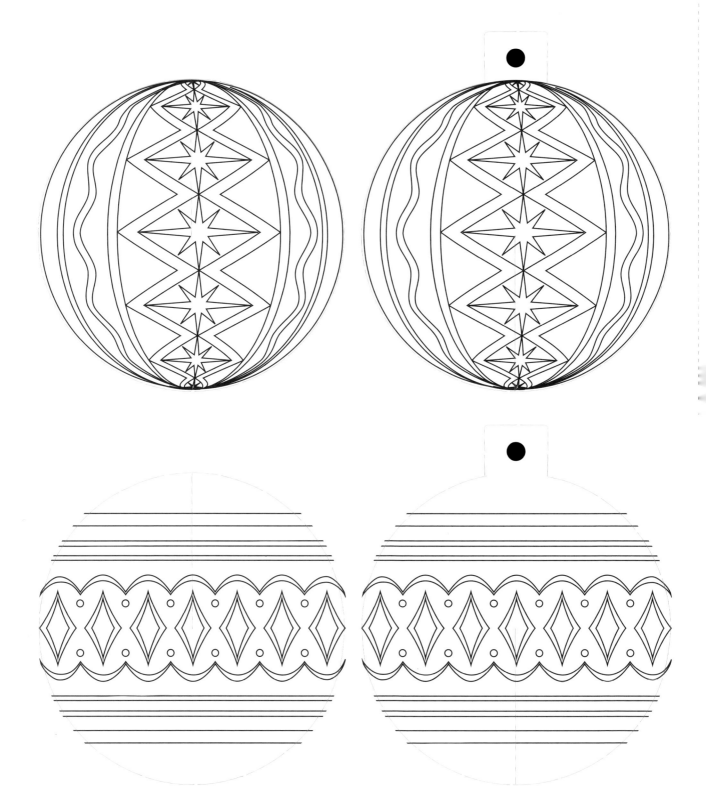

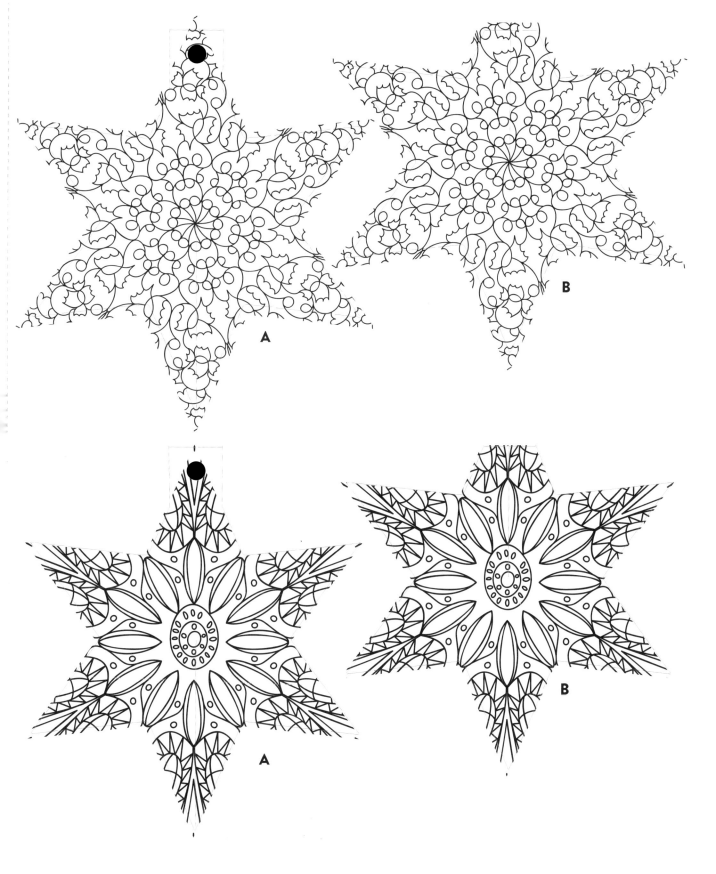

A

B

A

B

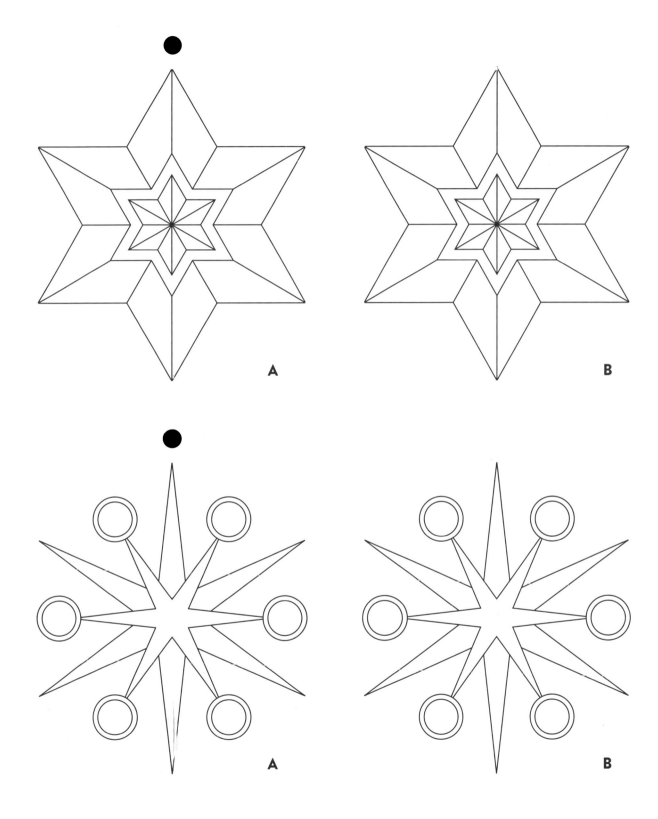

A

B

A

B

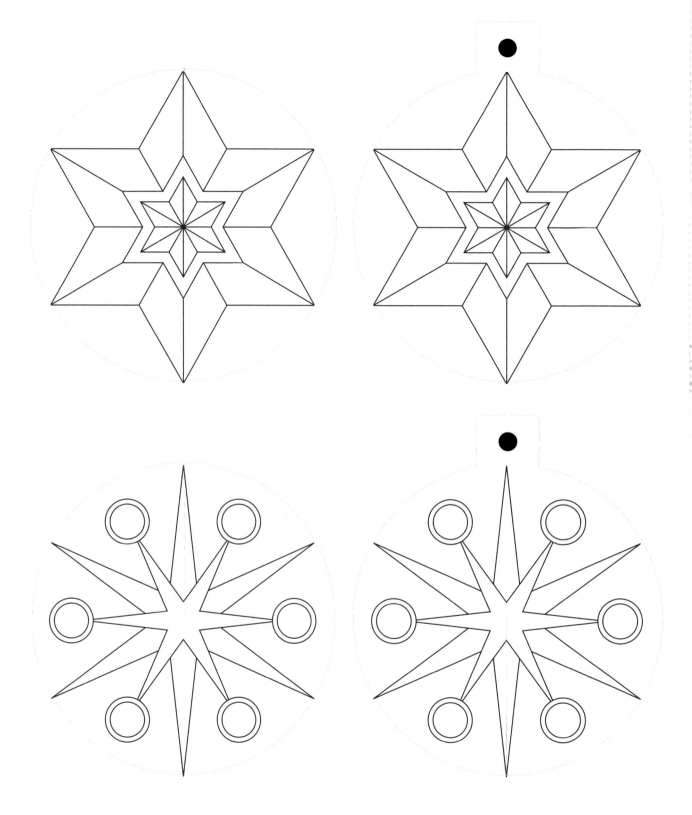

A

B

A

B

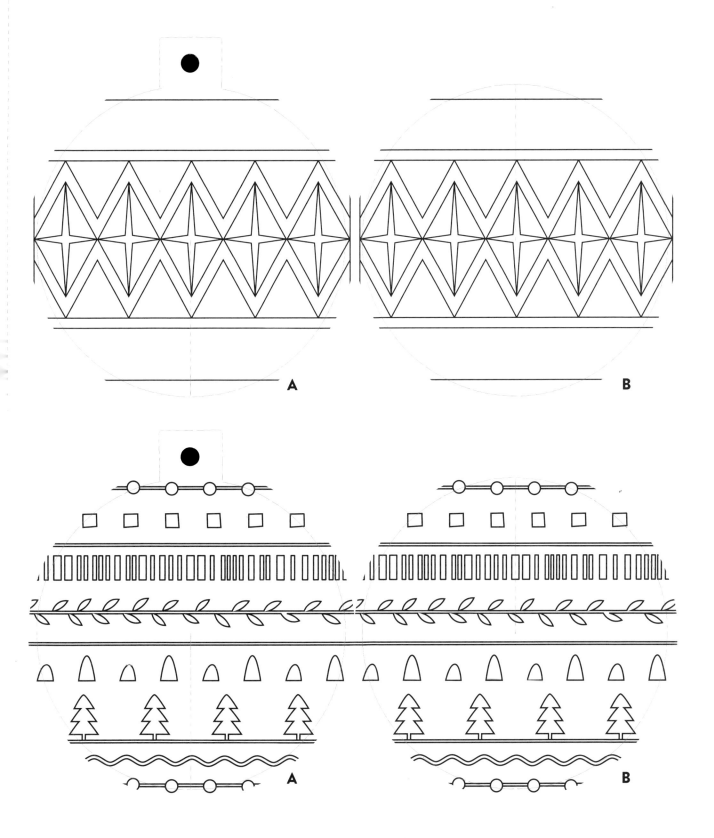

A

B

A

B

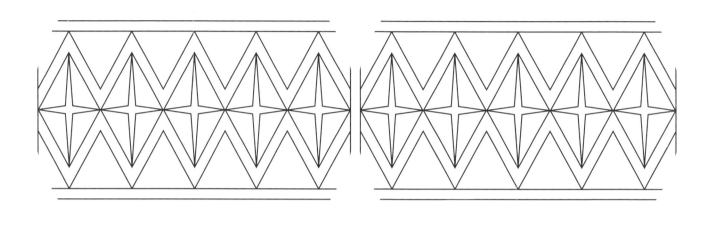

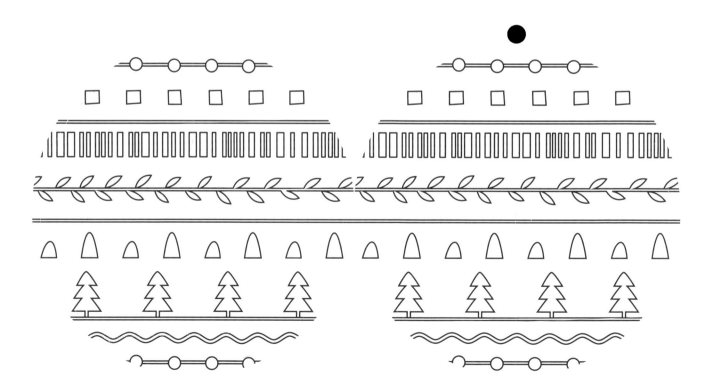

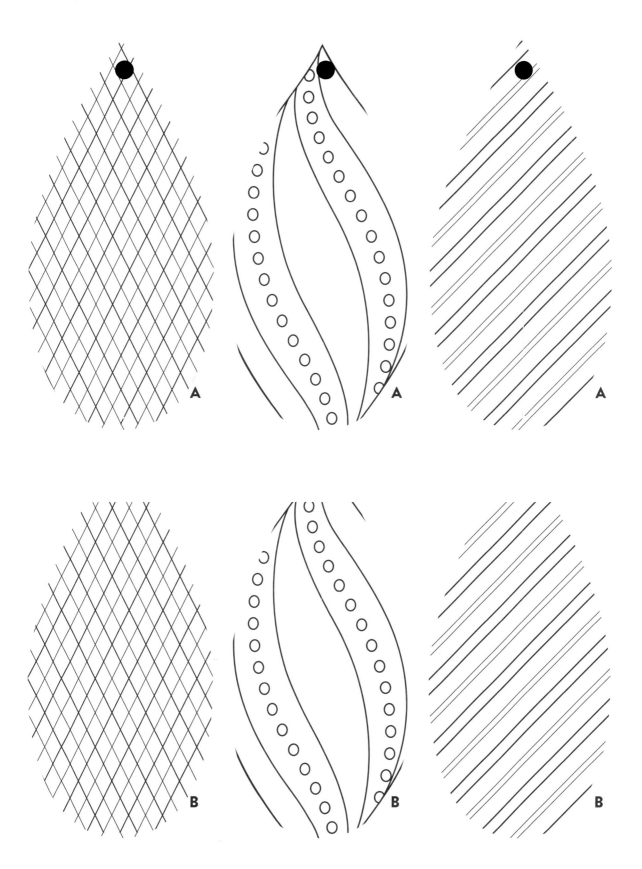

A

A

A

B

B

B

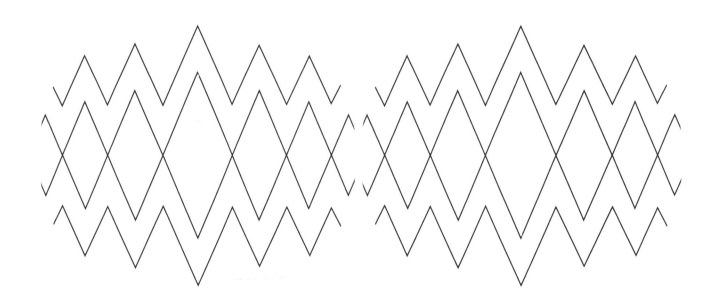